Spiri

Spiritual Maturity

A Journey through the Sinai with Jamie Buckingham

This book was taken from Jamie Buckingham's 13-part video Bible study series titled *The Journey to Spiritual Maturity*. The videos can be viewed for free at www.JamieBuckinghamMinistries.com.

Risky Living Ministries, Inc.

Spiritual Maturity: A Journey through the Sinai with Jamie Buckingham
By Jamie Buckingham
Edited by Bruce and Michele Buckingham

Copyright © 2017 by Risky Living Ministries, Inc.

Unless otherwise noted, scripture quotes are taken from THE HOLY BIBLE, NEW INTERNATIONAL VERSION®, NIV® Copyright © 1973, 1978, by Biblica, Inc.® Used by permission. All rights reserved worldwide.

Published by Risky Living Ministries, Inc.
3901 Hield Road NW
Palm Bay, FL 32907

www.RiskyLivingMinistries.com

Risky Living Ministries is dedicated to preserving the teachings and life works of Jamie Buckingham.

Cover photo (1976) of Jamie Buckingham resting on Mount Sinai by Bruce Buckingham

ISBN-13: 978-1544622538

Table of Contents

Chapter 1

Introduction to the Sinai

Everyone wants to grow up, to mature. Yet growth, especially spiritual growth, comes only through struggle and sometimes crisis. It's the baby chick trying to break out of the egg. It's the butterfly struggling to escape from the cocoon. It's the child struggling through adolescence towards the promised land of adulthood. But growth doesn't stop with adulthood. It continues on to the day we die, and perhaps beyond, because the call of God is always upward and onward. Jesus commanded His followers to grow spiritually: "Be perfect (or spiritually mature), as your Father in heaven is perfect" (Matthew 5:48).

Paul said that we should grow up into Jesus. In Romans, he said we should not stop growing until we are conformed to the image of Christ.

Such growth comes only by struggle. It's often accompanied by discouragement and despair. Why can't I reach my goal? Why do I have to keep wandering in this wilderness?

The path to spiritual maturity, spiritual growth, is a wilderness path. It strongly parallels the path taken by Moses and the children of Israel 3,200 years ago as they took their exodus from Egypt and entered the burning crucible of the Sinai on their way towards that Promised Land. Throughout this book, we're going to study the journey to spiritual maturity by tracing the footsteps of Moses.

On my last journey to the wilderness, I took a small group of 12 men with me. We camped out, cooked our own food, and slept under the stars. We traveled in two jeeps with Egyptian drivers and a seasoned Israeli guide. We stopped at strategic places along the way, and I taught the lessons that the children of Israel learned 3,200 years ago — lessons we need to learn on our own journey to spiritual maturity.

My prayer is that that this book will provide you with an opportunity to understand more about what God was saying when He spoke to those ancient Israelites. Consider it a sort of a journal of an journey we are taking together. So come with me, now, across the years, to the wilderness.

The time: approximately 1,200 years before the birth of Jesus Christ. The place: the Sinai Peninsula, that barren and remote desert which separated Egypt from the Promised Land of Israel. Into this burning crucible, Moses led the children of Israel. They were on foot fleeing the bondage of Egypt, where they had spent the last 480 years. They were on their way to claiming their inheritance, a land they had never seen, a land flowing with milk and honey. They were heading toward the land where the covenant God had made with their ancient ancestor, Abraham, would be fulfilled. It was the land that is still called by their name, the land of Israel.

I've been in this Sinai for a number of days now, this place that Moses called the great and terrible wilderness. I literally followed the footsteps of that band of Israelites as they trekked their way from Egypt towards the Promised Land. Here, I find nature in its rawest form, a Sinai that remains today as it was in the time of Moses, a scorching crucible which melts armies and burns from proud men all sin and selfishness until they are prepared for ministry.

The desert is a place of training, a place of preparation. Most of us don't like to train. We prefer to get out on the playing field. And yet, it's in the desert that we learn and grow towards spiritual maturity. It's there we learn to throw off everything that hinders us, the sin that does so easily entangle us. We learn to run with perseverance the race that is marked for us. It's there we fix our eyes on Jesus, the author and finisher of our faith.

In my own personal exodus from Egypt moving toward the Promised Land, I have struggled with spiritual growth. There's a tendency to want to withdraw and move back into caves like those hermits of early centuries. Yet God says, "Move on, move on." And so I've attempted to do that.

I went back into the Sinai time and time again, traveling with a group of men, each one of us on our own spiritual journey; believing that if we could follow the footsteps of

Moses, we would be able to find where God intended us to be at the same time — finding these mountains, moving upward, moving onward, tracing his path.

We begin our search on the eastern borders of Egypt, the place where the Suez Canal now joins the Gulf of Suez, the northern extension of the Red Sea. It was there, at a place called the *Yam-Suph*, or Sea of Reeds, that God sent a mighty east wind to blow back the waters and allow Moses to walk through on dry ground. From there, we're going to proceed south, stopping at a place called the Springs of Marah to learn something of purging. Then we'll move on again towards that wonderful oasis of Elim, where the Bible said that there were 70 palm trees and 12 springs. It's a place of God's filling, a place of God's provision.

We'll study how and why Moses brought water from the rock. And we'll climb the mountain at Rephidim, where Moses held up his staff while Joshua led his troops against the fierce Amalekites in the valley below. We'll journey on to Mount Sinai, *Jebel Musa* as the Arabs call it — the mountain of Moses — where God gave Moses the law. Along the way, we'll visit some exciting places, such as the oldest existing monastery in the world, Saint Catherine's Monastery, at the base of Mount Sinai. It was there, by the way, that former Egyptian premier, Anwar Sadat, built his desert retreat house.

We'll stop at a Bedouin graveyard and talk a little bit about hospitality. There, we'll see the tomb of a Bedouin sheikh. We'll let these strange desert nomads, the Bedouins, fix bread for us, the original *matzah,* or unleavened bread of the Passover. Eventually, we'll wind up at Kadesh-Barnea in the northern Sinai, where the Israelites learned their final lessons before entering Canaan.

I keep asking myself, "Why do I return to the desert? Why not to the mountains or to the seashore? Why the desert, with its scorching sands and craggy mountains?"

Emerging from the dark night of my soul several years ago, when it seemed I had almost destroyed myself and my own family, I determine to trace the literal path of those early searchers of promise, returning to the Sinai again and again across these years. I've begun to understand that there is indeed some kind of way through the wilderness. That which Moses did, I can do also. This wilderness still remains a place of purification, a place of preparation, a place where a man can learn to distinguish between the clamoring voices of this world and the often quiet, gentle voice of God.

That's why I return.

*   *   *   *   *

You find the desert really is your friend. There are trails in the desert, a way through the desert, so to speak. A man can stay alive here all of his life, if he knows where to find water and what to eat — and if he's not afraid of making friends with the inhabitants who live here. These strange, warm, friendly Bedouins are from a different culture, a different religion than most of us. Their concept of hospitality is to reach out. And if you reach back, they'll accept you as one of their own. There's no need to be afraid. Man really is afraid only of the unknown. But once you learn the wilderness — once you learn what we call dark is really light — there's no need to fear it anymore.

The secret to understanding the passage through the Sinai are the *wadis*. Wadis are huge, dry river beds that run between the high mountains crisscrossing the Sinai Peninsula. We left the Gulf of Eilat and turned inland through Wadi Watir, one of four major passageways across the Sinai Peninsula. We began to think about the passage of the children of Israel through this same Sinai Peninsula and especially their first stop at a place called Marah, which were the first springs that the children of Israel saw as they left the Gulf of Suez heading south towards Mount Sinai.

The children of Israel, with the Springs of Marah behind them, staggered through the desert sands along the Gulf of Suez. Their thirst had returned as the days grew longer and hotter. Slowly, the great procession turned inland following the directions of Moses, who had been this way many times before.

The desert brings out the very best and the very worst in men. For some reason, it's the place that God has always required His special people to go into. Moses was forced into the desert after his experience with the murdering of the Egyptian taskmaster. For 40 years he was in this place, this Sinai. It became a crucible for Moses. Here, he was ground into powder. And yet, out of that powder, God created — or perhaps recreated — a new man.

I think about that every time I come to this wilderness place. The mountains tower into the sky like a giant canopy overhead. And yet here, in the midst of all the silence, there's a still, small voice. That voice spoke to the prophet Elijah, and it speaks to me.

Perhaps the best word to describe the Sinai is mystery. It's fraught with mysterious experiences, and it's difficult to separate fable from the truth. It all gets blended together here in this mixture of sand and stone, stars and sky, and these rugged stone mountains.

We started our trek through the Plain of el-Raha, which is the great plain that spreads out before the base of Mount Sinai. It was here the children of Israel camped while Moses, leaving the multitude, went up into the mountain. We crossed it in our vehicle and came to the base of Mount Sinai proper, where Saint Catherine's Monastery is now located.

There is an interesting history behind Saint Catherine's. In the time of the Crusades, when the iconoclast came through tearing down all the icons, Saint Catherine's was spared. So it remains even today, perhaps the most famous monastery in the world — certainly the oldest monastery still in existence.

We left Saint Catherine's after a brief visit and began the arduous climb up Mount Sinai itself, *Jebel Musa*, the mountain of Moses. It towers almost 7,500 feet above sea level.

Climbing from Saint Catherine's, we made our way up through Saint Stephen's Gate. Again, tradition and fable seem all mixed up together. Saint Stephen built this gate with his own hands — a high arch over the steps — to examine all the pilgrims who came up the path to the summit of Mount Sinai. And so Saint Stephen, or Stephanus, sat beside his gate until he died. The sarcophagus now resides in the charnel house below at Saint Catherine's Monastery.

The wilderness does not have to be a place of hopeless fear and utter despair. Despite the hard lessons learned, the taste of bitter water, the conflict with self, nature, and desert enemies, it can be a place of tranquil beauty, perfect rest, and warm fellowship with fellow pilgrims. To bypass the wilderness on our journey to the Promised Land is to bypass God.

As our group was climbing Mount Sinai, we spotted far off in the distance a large wooden cross overlooking a deep valley below. As we approached the cross, we saw that far over the edge of the precipice, 2,500 feet below, was Saint Catherine's Monastery. Our men were eager to climb the hill, but our Jewish guide reminded us, "Be careful. Keep your eyes on the cross. Because if you don't, your feet will surely slip, and you'll plummet into the valley below." Perhaps that's God's message to those of us who are wandering in the wilderness: To make sure that your feet don't slip, keep your eye on the cross.

I wonder if I will return to this place again. It's been exciting — walking the places where Moses walked, meeting the people that still live here, remnants of those ancient Israelites. It's been exciting, in search of God. It's been exciting, an experiment in relationships. But for all that it's worth, I have found that God does not really reside in desert places. God resides wherever man's heart is turned to Him. To come here has been a respite, a time away. But it's not real.

So I must return. I must return to my family. I must return to my friends. I must return to the church that I belong to. I must return to my job. For it's there where God is. It's there where I must live with Him and obey His commands.

You do not have to come to the Sinai. You do not have to come to the wilderness to find Him. True, God has been here, and we still see His footprints in many places. But how much better it is for those who follow His footprints in the place where they live, rather than coming to what *used* to be holy ground. How much better it is to find Him where you are.

Jamie Buckingham

Chapter 2

Purging: The Waters of Marah

The wilderness. The term itself brings forth images of lostness, wandering, despair. But that doesn't have to be the case.

The children of Israel first crossed the desert journeying from Egypt, where they'd been slaves for many generations, to a land promised them by God. That was more than 3,200 years ago. For them, the desert was a place of wandering and lostness. But because their leader, Moses, recorded their journey in that wonderful book called the Bible, we're now able to learn God's plan for our life — His plan for spiritual maturity.

You know, we're all on a journey from the place of bondage — life lived without God — to a place called spiritual maturity. Let's learn from those ancient pilgrims. By the time we finish this journey, each one of us should be experiencing some degree of increasing spiritual maturity — knowing God, loving God and accepting His love for us.

We're going to follow the footsteps of Moses and his band of Israelites from the eastern shore of the Yam Suph, *the legendary Red Sea, to the borders of Canaan, which is still occupied today by the Israelis. That journey took the Israelites of old 40 years. We'll not take that long. But I believe that as we cross that desert and learn some lessons from God, we too can experience spiritual maturity and find power for living.*

I'm going to take you to some remote places in the Sinai where the children of Israel learned some particularly significant lessons about God and about life. I had with me, when I made my trips, a small group of friends. We traveled by jeep to each location. When we stopped, I taught. I invite you to go with us and learn some of the significant lessons first taught by God to that wandering band of Israelites.

The first stop on our journey to spiritual maturity is, of all things, a potty stop. Following their miraculous deliverance from the Red Sea, the Israelites moved rapidly towards the land of Canaan. But God spoke and said they were not to follow the shore of the Mediterranean. Instead of going directly to Canaan, they were first to go south, which is in the opposite direction, along the eastern shore of the Gulf of Suez. For three days they traveled. Then their water ran out. Their throats were parched. They were dying of thirst. But God was leading them, and soon they spotted ahead a marvelous oasis — Marah. It is here that I shared this first significant lesson to be learned in our journey toward spiritual maturity.

The very first place the children of Israel stopped when they came out of Egypt was the pools of Marah. Actually, the word itself means "bitter," but they didn't know it was bitter. They'd gone for three days without anything to drink. Their throats were dry. Then, they found this marvelous oasis with palm trees and flat rocks. They came rushing toward it with all of their cattle, yearning to get something to drink. But when they knelt down to taste the water, they found out that it was laced with magnesium and calcium. It was impossible to drink. The water was too bitter. So they grumbled and complained against Moses.

Moses, wise to the ways of the desert, went through a procedure of taking hold of a particular bush and throwing it into the water. This caused the chemicals in the bitter waters to precipitate to the bottom of the pool. Soon, the water in that pool was sweet and drinkable.

But the whole issue here brings up a question: Did God know that this water was bitter? Did God know ahead of time what lay ahead for those children of Israel for three days? They were without water, and suddenly they came to the pools, but they couldn't drink it. It presents a challenging question: Is God in charge of our lives?

If you're like me, you've had a lot of experiences like this. How often have I gone rushing toward a beautiful pool of seemingly clean pure water, only to taste and find out I can't drink it? Does God know what's going on in my life?

As an old Bible scholar once said a long time ago, God is not only interested in getting the children of Israel out of

Egypt, He's also interested in getting Egypt out of the children of Israel. Egypt was a dirty place. They'd just been through a number of plagues. They had left Egypt after a terrible night, when thousands of first-born children had died. They'd come out of that place full of frogs and flies and locust and boils. And within a few days, they were in the desert of Sinai without water. How was God going to clean Egypt out of their system? Well, it looked like the best way to clean them out was to bring them to a place like Marah and to have them drink of the chemically-laced waters there.

As I said, the water at Marah is filled with magnesium and calcium. You can't see it in the water, but as it dries on your hands, you can feel it. It's oily. And if it dries completely, it leaves a fine dust — the dust of magnesium, the very chemical that we use today to clean out our digestive systems. It appeared that God did have a purpose after all in bringing the children of Israel to the waters of Marah.

I've had to drink a lot of bitter things in my life. I've had to drink from the bitter cup. Nobody likes to do it. It's the same kind of cup Jesus had to drink from when He went to the cross. In the garden of Gethsemane Jesus prayed,

> "My father, if it is possible, may this cup be taken from me. Yet not as I will, but as you will" (Matthew 26:39).

God has a lot of bitter water that He wants us to drink. But He's got a purpose behind it. We may not understand it, and our friends may not understand it, but God has a real purpose for our drinking the bitter waters.

The waters at Marah also contain an interesting chemical composition called dolomite. It's the same kind of chemical that doctors give athletes today to keep their heart muscles regulated and to keep the muscles in their body regulated in the hot sun. God not only wanted to clean out the systems of the Israelites; but He also wanted to make them strong and healthy for what lay ahead.

Because He had a purpose for them, He was also going to change their appetites. He was going to put them on a kosher food diet and teach them how to eat properly for their desert existence. He was also going to teach them how to walk and how to live outside of Egypt. God wanted those children of Israel to live long lives. But eventually they failed in their most critical test.

We will learn more about their failures in the lessons to come. But for now, remember, we don't have to fail. If we drink the bitter waters that God has placed in front of us, we will live long, creative and productive lives, all for the glory of God.

Jamie Buckingham

Chapter 3

Provision: Filled with the Spirit

In our journey towards spiritual maturity, it's mandatory that we learn early on that God can be trusted. He takes care of His children. Even when we're ignorant, disobedient and faithless, God is faithful.

The children of Israel left Egypt in the middle of the Jewish month of Nisan, which pretty well corresponds to the middle of April. Turning south along the Gulf of Suez, they marched until their water ran out at Marah. There they learned the lesson of purging.

From Marah they continued south, heading toward Mt. Sinai, the same mountain where Moses had encountered God at the burning bush. Remember, Moses had been that way many times before during the 40 years that he lived in the desert, herding sheep and goats for his father-in-law, Jethro.

The lesson we are going to learn next is the lesson of provision. The Israelites were trudging south towards Elam, a place described in the Bible as a place of 12 springs and

70 palm trees. But here's the thing: God is going to meet us at every corner. If you keep pushing forward, God will provide even at the last minute.

On the way to Elam, and scattered all throughout the Sinai, are Acacia trees. We rested near one. Remember, it was from the wood of the Acacia tree that Moses formed the Ark of the Covenant. This particular tree where we stopped was in the bottom of a huge wadi — a dry river bed or gulch, a deep canyon between two towering granite mountains. The roots of the tree had been exposed by the raging water which flows through there on rare occasion. It was there, near that tree, that I taught of putting your roots down and trusting in God's provision.

Nothing in the Sinai Desert can live for long on surface water alone. The water doesn't soak into the ground; it moves in a hurry. We are sitting now in the midst of a great wadi, with mountains on each side. Yet, in the midst of this is greenery. Consider the lowly Acacia tree. Its source of water is obviously underground. There is no surface water to be seen.

So many people come into the wilderness and feel that if they can find a pool of water to drink from, they can live. Our own personal wildernesses are like that. We're constantly looking for that which is obvious. And yet the real nourishment is under the ground. It's never found on the surface. The roots, like the roots of the Acacia tree, are the secret to the life and greenery of the tree. The spiritual man, David once said, is like a tree planted by rivers of water, that yields, or brings forth, its fruit in its season.

And yet, in the Sinai there are no streams of water. There is not a single river in all of the Sinai. There are just dry river beds, wadis. There will be times when it will rain in the desert. And when it does, the river beds will fill up quickly with the water rushing through the mountains towards the sea. Oftentimes, large piles of rock will be deposited at the roots of the Acacia tree. Many times the roots of the tree will be exposed due to the erosion.

As we consider the Acacia tree, the lesson for the spiritual man is very plain. The spiritual man does not need constant nourishment, or constantly flowing water. The spiritual man doesn't need to be watered every day. He prospers even when the skies are cloudless, even when the land is parched.

The marvelous Acacia tree provided the wood that the Ark of the Covenant was carved from in the Sinai. Its roots can extend as far as 50 feet into the ground. So, even though there are long periods of time when there is no surface water — sometimes years with no rain at all — this tree continues to flourish. It flourishes because it has put its roots down deep.

If the wilderness says anything to those of us who are wandering through it — whatever your wilderness may be — it says we need to put our roots down deep.

Drinking from the waters of the Nile was no longer available to the Israelites as they trekked through the Sinai.

Nor was it enough for them to grow spiritually. The children of Israel had to learn to put their roots down deep as the Acacia tree does. They needed to learn that there was health in always searching, always looking, for that which will constantly nourish from below the surface. They needed to learn to no longer be content to live on surface water, which can often be polluted; but rather, to live as a tree which lives by the rivers of living water, drawing forth from the deep, and therefore bearing fruit in its season.

The Acacia tree, gnarled and stubby as it is, can live up to 200 years, constantly putting forth green shoots for its entire life. If you look high into the branches, you will see the little yellow blossoms. To be sure, there are thorns, and it's not very beautiful to look at. Yet, God chose this tree to be the container for the most holy thing that Moses would build: the Ark of the Covenant.

For each one of us who are pilgrims, we need to learn to put our roots down. Job said it best, many, many years ago:

> "At least there is hope for a tree: If it is cut down, it will sprout again, and its new shoots will not fail. Its roots may grow old in the ground and its stump die in the soil, yet at the scent of water it will bud and put forth shoots like a plant" (Job 14:7-9).

Chapter 4

Obedience: Water from the Rock

We've been tracing our own journey of spiritual maturity by following the footsteps of Moses and that band of former slaves as they made their way out of Egypt and through the wilderness. The stops we make as we journey through the wilderness mark significant milestones in our own pilgrimage towards spiritual maturity.

For instance, after that wonderful miracle at the Red Sea — the Yam Suph, which is really the northern part of the Gulf of Suez — we followed the footsteps of the Israelites to the bitter waters of Marah. There, we learned of the necessity of being purged of all of our old life. From there we moved on, following the children of Israel as they went trudging through the desert sand, coming to the beautiful place of Elim. There we paused at an Acacia tree and learned of God's faithful provision.

Now, we'll learn the lesson of obedience.

Rain in the Sinai is rare. In fact, the average rainfall in the Southern Sinai is less than one inch a year. But when it does rain, it's often torrential. In fact, sometimes the desert may go five years without any rain, and then have all five inches fall in one night. That's awesome!

One afternoon, I crawled up on a rock — the same kind of rock that Moses struck with his staff to bring forth water. I talked to my companions and taught them about Moses striking the rock — and about obedience.

The Sinai is a barren place. There are no rivers, no forest, no meadows, no plains. Just bare rock and boulders and sand, and only a few plants adapted to the harsh conditions of the desert. Sometimes the desert will go five years without any kind of rain. Then, when it does rain, it's torrential, and it may see five inches fall in one night. It's an awesome sight when that happens.

During those occasional flash floods, an extraordinary event may take place. A great wall of water comes raging down through the wadis, sometimes as high as 30 feet. It exerts great force on the walls of the canyon. At the places where igneous and sedimentary rock come together in the sides of the mountains, the water can carve out great fissures, creating a vast reservoir holding thousands or perhaps millions of gallons of water. After the floods pass, the water begins to seep from its rocky mountain reservoir. Calcium deposits quickly form around the opening, sealing off the water inside the rock.

As winter snows melt on the highest mountaintops, water percolates through the ground and comes forth in other places as springs. Sometimes, it'll be absorbed into the ground and reappear further down the wadi as a creek. At other times, however, it remains trapped inside the rock fissures.

Once I watched a Bedouin shepherd, in an action called a *timile*, take his staff and strike the rock at exactly the right spot. He broke loose the calcium deposits, allowing water to gush forth. This was the same thing Moses did when he was faced with a water emergency right here near this place.

The children of Israel, taking their trek inland, noticed how the scenery had begun to change. The burning sands gave way to massive, granite formations. There was no vegetation, no skin to cover the skeleton of the mountains themselves. I imagine that the people were walking silently, wondering where in the world they were going to find water in these high mountain places.

The scenery was breathtaking, but at the same time it was a terrible situation to be in. As the sun reflected off the towering peak of Mount Sinai, which lay ahead, the people knew they were going to walk through a very high mountain pass, a deep cleft in the rock, with granite mountains on each side.

Questions kept coming from all the people: "Where are we going to find water, Moses?" Despite the awe they felt in that majestic place, they began to grumble.

The Bible says the whole Israelite community finally camped at Rephidim. But there was no water for the people. So, they did what you and I do. They quarreled. They grumbled. "Give us water to drink," they cried. But Moses rebuked them, saying they weren't doubting his ability; they were doubting God's ability.

Thirst does strange things to people. It drives them into panic. So these folks began to murmur and grumble. As they had done at Marah, they mumbled here at Rephidim, as well: "Why did you bring us here so that we would die without water?"

Moses remembered the place. He had been there before. Surely there'd be a water reservoir behind these rock walls. So moving on ahead of the people, he gently began tapping the rock walls with his staff until he found a soft spot. Then telling everyone to run and fetch their water containers, he took his staff and, with a mighty blow, struck of the rock. And water came forth.

People thought it was a miracle, and indeed it was. But you see, the *timile* was something Moses had done many times before. But for the Israelites, it was a new occurrence.

The people were getting ready to lose respect for their leader. They didn't know what God had in store. They didn't know that in the coming days a great event was going to take place, and they needed to know Moses was in authority. God allowed Moses to get the credit by bringing water from the rock, so that God would get the glory for the events that were to follow.

Forty years later Moses would be faced with a similar challenge. It happened at Kadesh Barnea, many miles to the north. Once again, the Israelites were without water. As he had done years before at Rephidim, Moses came before the Lord and said, "God, where are we going to find water?" God said, "Take your staff, gather the people, then speak to the rock, and it'll pour out its water."

But a subtle change had taken place in Moses across the years. Earlier in his life, he had been a man who had listened keenly to God and had adjusted immediately. He was a man of daring, venturesome faith.

But now Moses had grown old. His ways were set. He no longer welcomed change. He resisted change by fleeing to the safe harbor of tradition. Moses was no longer a new wineskin. He had grown old, and his wineskin was dry and cracked. And his spirit, although faithful to God, had lost its elasticity. He was no longer willing to expand. It was easier to do as he had done in the past than to venture out and attempt something new, even though God had commanded it.

And so, instead of speaking to the rock, Moses reverted to the time-tested procedure of the *timile*. He struck the rock as he had done before at Rephidim. Not only that, but he struck it with bitterness and with anger. Water came forth, of course.

Humanistic knowledge may produce results. Although Moses brought forth water, he did it in his own strength. And that was displeasing to God. As a result of his disobedience, Moses was declared disqualified by God to lead the children of Israel into the Promised Land.

You see, Moses had lost his willingness to change. It was a sad day. The old leader was no longer able to lead. The nation of Israel now required a new, young leader who would obey and follow God. That's the lesson of obedience. If Moses would not obey God at Kadesh Barnea, what would he do when he got to the Jordan River?

The wilderness lessons are stark, but they must be learned if we are going to move on to spiritual maturity.

Here, then, are the lessons of obedience: What worked yesterday is not sufficient for today. God's word yesterday must be adjusted by God's word today. To be tyrannized by the past is the worst of all tyrannies. The rut of tradition is but one step removed from the graves in the wilderness. God's word to His pilgrims is fresh every morning. It's a lamp to our feet and a light to our path. The man who trusts in God will never be embarrassed or defeated.

Chapter 5

Authority: Coming into Submission

In our journey through the wilderness, we've stopped along the way to learn some valuable lessons on the subject of spiritual maturity. We've gleaned them from the experiences of the ancient Israelites as they walked through that same place 3200 years ago. Like us, they were on their way from bondage to freedom, from spiritual infancy to spiritual maturity. That involves responsibility and eventually learning authority. God taught them as He often teaches us: through literal experiences.

He brought them from the waters of the Red Sea, where they experienced a great miracle, to a place of desolation at the waters of Marah. From there they traveled to the beautiful oasis of Elim, where they found out about God's loving provision. Then, on to the valley of Rephidim, where Moses struck the rock. At that place, God was setting the stage for what was going to happen the next day. It was important that these former slaves learned the truth of submission and authority, because the next day the Israelites were going to face a challenge that they had never faced before — and it was not lack of water. They were going to be attacked by a fierce band of blood-thirsty cave dwellers, desert terrorists called Amalekites.

These Amalekites lived in the lush valley of Rephidim. They, the Bible says, had no fear, not even of God. But the Israelites had to go through them. The Amalekites were angry because the Israelites were coming in their direction. War was inevitable.

God told Moses to climb a small mountain overlooking the valley of Rephidim. There, along with his brother Aaron and his cousin Hur, he would stretch out his hands in intercession while his young captain, Joshua, led the Israelites into battle in the valley below.

On my last journey to the Sinai, I climbed that same mountain, a natural overview called Mount Tahuna. It towers almost a thousand feet over the valley below. On the summit are the remnants of a small chapel built more than a thousand years ago by pilgrims. It was there I talked to my small group about authority.

The weight of authority on the spiritual leader is far more than most people realize. When Moses got to this place, a valley called Rephidim, suddenly they came face to face with the first major battle that the children of Israel had had. Living in caves all through this area were barbarians — a cave people called the Amalekites, who were followers of Amalek, a barbarian chief. The Amalekites refused to let the children of Israel pass through this valley, which was necessary for them to traverse in order to arrive at Mount Sinai, the mountain of God.

So a great battle took place in this valley. The Amalekites were trained soldiers, barbarians. The children of Israel were former slaves. They had never been in a battle before. But God had a battle plan for His people. He told Moses to rise early in the morning and climb to the top of Mount Tahuna, which overlooked the valley of Rephidim. And while he was there, he told Joshua, his young warrior, to lead the troops of Israel into battle against the Amalekites in the valley below.

But it was more than just a battle plan, for God had something else in mind. He wanted Moses to come and stand on top of this mountain in the role of an intercessor. The place of leadership is far more than just one who raises the sword and raises the banner; the leader also has to be an intercessor on behalf of his people. So Moses stood on top of that mountain, standing between man below fighting the battle and God above, interceding on behalf of his friends, his followers.

The rod, or staff, which had been Moses' constant companion, was to be held out over that valley. In fact, the Scriptures say that as long as the rod was extended over the valley, the battle went in favor of Israel. Only when Moses' arms grew weary and he dropped the rod did the battle go in favor of the Amalekites. So Moses stood as an intercessor between the people below and God above, so the battle would go in favor of his followers.

Jesus is our intercessor. He stands between us and God. We really don't have to do any fighting down here on this earth. That's for religious people. But for those of us who have known the fullness of God's Spirit, we understand that we have a great intercessor who stands above us on the mountaintop, who fights all of our battles for us. Jesus and the angels of heaven are actually doing the fighting for us in the heavenly places. All we have to do is cooperate with God, obey Him, and walk in His decrees as He sets them forth.

Another thing happened that morning while the battle was raging and the day grew longer. Holding his staff above his head as God had commanded, Moses' arms began to grow weary. He wasn't able to hold them up for very long. The Bible says that Aaron and Hur, Moses' brother and brother-in-law, came and helped him hold his arms up so that the battle could go favorably in the direction of the Israelites rather than in the direction of the Amalekites.

This is a perfect example of how we need one another. No leader can actually do his job completely unless his friends are around him to give him assistance and encouragement, like Aaron and Hur helped Moses.

Chapter 6

Changed Appetites:
Manna from Heaven

It's hard to imagine what it would be like to have the same breakfast every morning for 40 years, and the same stuff for lunch — then to have it again in the evening. But for 40 years, the Israelites lived off of one basic food — manna.

In this lesson from the Sinai, I teach about changed appetites. I will describe some fascinating man-made structures, some of the oldest in the world still standing today. They're called nawamis, *circular stone tombs. Many experts believe that they are the original "graves of craving," where the Israelites were buried after they stuffed themselves on quail. But it wasn't overeating that killed the Israelites. It was their attitude of thanklessness and complaining.*

Come with me as I teach in the Sinai, and as we move toward spiritual maturity — hopefully, learning the lesson of changed attitudes and changed appetites.

The first encounter with manna came when the Israelites ran out of food after leaving Elim on the way to Mount Sinai. There had been some more complaining in the camp. God seemed to understand and said to Moses, "I will rain down bread from heaven." It was another remarkable and miraculous evidence of God's love and care for His people. At the same time quail appeared. This was a special bonus of meat for the people. It was the first time they'd had meat since leaving Egypt. But when the quail did not reappear as often as the steady diet of manna did, the people complained.

Every morning, despite the fact that it was God's divine provision for the Israelites, the people said they were tired of the same diet. And again, after leaving Mount Sinai on their way to Kadesh-Barnea, they began to grumble. This time, however, God acted sternly. Moses had earlier warned the people about grumbling. He told them, "You're not grumbling against me. You're grumbling against God." But the people turned a deaf and rebellious ear to God's warning, and God said, "I am going to act."

At a place called the Graves of Craving, the quail again appeared by the thousands. This time, instead of giving God the praise, the people rushed out and stuffed themselves on the quail. And God's wrath fell on them. While they were gorging themselves, thousands of them died. Today, scattered all across the Sinai, are strange round gravesites made of stone called *nawamis*.

Archaeologists say that these freestanding stone structures are the oldest existing above-ground structures in all the world. Although, they've long since been looted by robbers and archaeologists, when first discovered, they were filled with human bones. Tradition says they were the bones of the grumblers who were discontented with God's provision of manna and lusted after the flesh pots of Egypt.

The tragedy of human history is that man never seems to learn from his mistakes, or the mistakes of those who've gone before him. The person who insists upon learning everything from personal experience will seldom make progress. At worst he's going to perish in the wilderness. The wise pilgrim, on his way to spiritual maturity, builds and learns from the past.

The human heart is the same in all generations. Satan has no new tactics. When the Apostle Paul was writing to the church in Corinth about the events that happened to the children of Israel in the Sinai, he warned the Corinthians not to repeat history. Paul listed the things that the Israelites did to displease God: idolatry, revelry, sexual immorality, grumbling. It's significant to understand that Paul lists grumbling as an equal way to displease God, right along with pagan revelry and sexual immorality.

There's a school of thought that says it's all right to curse at God, to get whatever is bothering you off your chest. But such an attitude assumes that God never responds to man's objections. The wilderness wanderings teach us otherwise.

God has a purpose for everything that He does. There was a purpose in the manna, as there was in the bitter springs at

Marah. He wanted to purge their systems. His next part in the plan was to change their diet. But as at Marah, the people rebelled. They failed to see that God had a master plan for their life, and nothing was left to chance. Had the Israelites stopped to think, they would have understood that God was pledged by the most solemn of obligations to provide for them. Instead, they grumbled because they did not believe.

Remember, Jesus was unable to work miracles in Nazareth because of their unbelief. So, also, the Israelites missed God's best plan for them by grumbling. The sin of unbelief is the greatest of all sins. Manna was not what they wanted on God's menu. They wanted the food of Egypt. But God's ways are not our ways. His provision often looks superficial to the common life. But we are God's chosen people.

Still, we complain. "Why do we have to have such a meager diet? We should have the food of kings, like the pharaohs." But that's the sin of presumption. The Israelites felt they knew better than God. They felt they knew better what they needed to eat. They were too short-sighted to understand that God wanted to close the door to Egypt's food. God was more interested in teaching them obedience than in satisfying their carnal cravings.

Temptation, which in its basic form is always a desire to return to Egypt, demands a tempter, one who stimulates our minds away from God. The tempter in this case was the many Egyptians who had been invited to join the Exodus, but they were not part of the covenant group. The Bible calls them the rabble, or the mixed multitude. The problem with mixed multitudes is differing appetites. Appetites are determined largely by family, and the Egyptians yearned for leeks and onions and melons. Moses, who had spent the last 40 years in this wilderness, was profoundly grateful for even just a little manna from heaven.

When Moses refused to listen to the grumbling people and their request to turn back, the people rebelled. This was a counter-revolution. It's the same thing all counter-revolutionaries face. They grew discouraged. They didn't like the diet, and on their long trek to the Promised Land, they felt they needed more. But God was changing their appetite. He was transforming a group of sloppy, undisciplined former slaves into an army.

There's no place for gourmet menus in the desert. In this desert, men must learn to exist on bare essentials. They don't live off of what fills their bellies. They live off of faith.

I remember a trip I made into the Sinai years ago. I brought my son, Bruce, with me. In fact, we got to this very place, and he was having trouble adapting to the rigors of desert living. After a while he began to talk about what he really wanted: an ice-cold Coke. The Israeli guide was amused at this American way of life, and began to point out the dangers of carbonated drinks.

"It tickles the throat and fools you into thinking that your body has been satisfied," she said. "But you don't drink to satisfy your throat. You drink to replenish the liquid that the sun has dehydrated out of your body."

The same principle works in the spiritual area as well. The manna of God was only meant to be temporary. Just a few days ahead lay the Promised Land with milk and wine and honey. But because of disobedience, because of their refusal to trust God, they had to live off of manna for 40 years.

The carnal appetite which God was trying to burn out of them had a hard time dying. You see, their throats had been tickled by the leeks and onions of Egypt, and they yearned for more. They ran after every new thing that came along. They were willing to trade in the written word of God for that which was more palatable. They demanded melons and onions from Egypt while disdaining what God has placed before them.

The only way to reach spiritual maturity is by eating God's diet. Leeks and onions and garlic will not take you into Canaan, for that diet is always accompanied by the bondage of Egypt. In the wilderness, we must make priority decisions. Are we willing to give up that which satisfies the belly in order to have that which satisfies the soul?

Those who ignore or refuse God's plan while wanting the former things must eventually be put away, the Bible says. They'll perish and be buried in the sands of the wilderness. Yet those who accept God's meager diet, believing God has a purpose for what he offers, will enter into a marvelous relationship, understanding that the manna is but for a season.

For those who obey and do not grumble, they have the table in the wilderness. Here then is the truth: while we are *in* the wilderness, we're not *of* the wilderness. We're bound for a Promised Land of spiritual maturity.

Jamie Buckingham

Chapter 7

Restoration: Spiritual Dominion

I have a staff that has become like an old friend. It's made of hickory from a tree in North Carolina. Moses had a staff like mine. It was probably made of Acacia wood. And it was his constant companion.

I've carried my staff to the Sinai on several occasions. No, I've never used it to open the sea or bring water out of a rock like Moses did. But it has helped me climb mountains, trudge through the deep sand, and one time it protected me from a deadly carpet viper. Likewise, my silver knife, which an old Bedouin gave me, is a precious keepsake. I love them both. They speak to me of restoration. The knife was fashioned from a piece of a junked automobile. My staff, filled with knot holes, came from a dead tree.

As we move onward to spiritual maturity, we'll learn that God loves to take junk and turn it into jewels. He loves to take a dead tree and help support life with it, as I am leaning on my staff. Join me again on one of my trips into the desert and learn an important lesson from the wilderness: the lesson of restoration.

When God needs a tool for service, he looks for common things to put into use. He doesn't reach for a knife that has been factory sharpened; rather, he prefers to choose rough metal and hone the blade himself. The Bedouin knife I have was not manufactured in an American factory. Rather, it was made by the Bedouins themselves. They crafted the handle from silver they mined with their own hands and made the blade from the metal off an old truck.

God does that in the wilderness. He chooses rough things and sharpens them for His own use. God chose a murderer many, many years ago. Moses, a man who had just finished a forty-year prison sentence in the desert, was chosen by God to lead His children out of Egypt and to a promised land. Instead of a golden scepter, Moses carried a wooden staff and, with God's power, transformed it into a rod of authority.

It's the principle of the transformed staff that we need to learn while here in the Sinai wilderness: transforming the secular into the sacred. God took a slingshot, an instrument that David had used for many years, and made it into a very special instrument to defeat a whole army of Philistines. He took a ram's horn, which became the great symbol of calling the people together. And remember, it was a lowly manger that God chose for His son to be born into this world. Later, the man, Jesus, took five loaves of bread and two fish from a little boy and miraculously fed 5,000 people. And who can forget that it was an old rugged cross that has become the symbol of all that's beautiful, yet it started as something that was very ugly, very common?

And so a simple rod that God pointed out to Moses became the great staff of authority. Perhaps it was the same rod that Moses had once used to kill the Egyptian taskmaster, the same one he then carried for all those years through his forced exile in the Sinai wilderness. It was his rod that became transformed when God said, "With this rod you will open seas. You will bring water from rocks. And the time will come when you hold it out over an entire valley, and the Amalekites will be defeated while Joshua rages war down below."

Earlier, Moses had used his rod as a symbol of physical force. So often we try to do that. We try to force our way through the kingdom of God. We try to force our way in by doing religious things. But it took the wilderness to purify Moses and to show him there was far more to following God than the use of force. So Moses carried a bloodstained rod, just as Jacob, who wrestled with God, walked with a limp from the rest of his life.

The rod of Moses was not perfect. No doubt it had knots in it, was twisted and bent. But God loves to use imperfect things — and people — for His purposes. He took the gnarled wood of an Acacia tree to house the ark of His presence. Likewise He took the staff of Moses — the same staff Moses had for years used to beat off the snakes and wild animals while tending his sheep and goats — to become the great symbol of authority.

The wilderness teaches us to be faithful in small things. God honors the person who will do that which He has put for his hands to do. God does not skip through our lives; rather, He says all things are important. Every day is important.

Even an imperfect staff, when touched by God, can become a great symbol of authority.

Chapter 8

The Call of God: The Burning Bush

Throughout this book I've been introducing you to new aspects of the journey towards spiritual maturity, as we follow the footsteps of Moses and his band of Israelites making their way across the Sinai towards the Promised Land.

Next, I want to talk to you about God's call. I want to flash back to the time when Moses first heard the call of God — at the burning bush. That happened near the base of Mount Sinai.

If we, like Moses, are to move towards spiritual maturity, we must be certain of God's call on our life. Here, near Mount Sinai, I shared with my friends who were traveling with me, what happened at that burning bush when God called Moses.

There are certain days in the lives of people that arrive unannounced. There are no heralded trumpets and no lightning flashes. They seem to be common, ordinary days. And yet, looking back on them, we find out that they're the most important and special days in our lives. Moses had one of these days. He'd been out in this wilderness for 40 years and had given up all thoughts of ever going back to Egypt, of ever having a place in Pharaoh's palace again.

He was simply doing the things that his hand found to do. He was herding sheep and goats for his father-in-law, Jethro. He was just doing the common things of everyday life. Then one day he was coming through a valley near the base of Mount Sinai. I can imagine him walking along tending his sheep, the sun coming up over the mountains, the sheep and goats foraging on the hillside. I can see Moses leaning back against his staff and resting, when he notices a phenomenon that has changed history — a bush was on fire.

It's not an unheard of thing to see a fire, especially in the Sinai, because sometimes a dry bush will catch the reflecting rays of the sun from the crystal-like rocks in the bottom of a wadi and burn. But this was an unusual fire because as he watched the bush burn, it was not consumed. It burned and burned and burned.

Moses had a lot of time on his hands. He never had free time in Egypt; but out here, in the desert, he had lots of time. So, not being in a hurry, Moses had time to turn aside and take a closer look at the bush. When he got closer, he heard a voice speak. It was the first time anyone had heard God's voice in 480 years. But God spoke and called Moses by name.

You may recall the poem from Elizabeth Barrett Browning:

> Earth's crammed with heaven,
> And every common bush afire with God,
> But only he who sees takes off his shoes;
> The rest sit round and pluck blackberries.

The problem with most of us is we're too busy. We're too busy to stop and inquire. We're too busy to get quiet and listen. And even if God called our name, we wouldn't be able to hear it because we're on the go too much.

Think about all those men in the Bible that God called, such as Gideon and Amos and Isaiah. They were all busy men, busy doing the things they were supposed to be doing. Every one of them was occupied with the small task that was at hand. And yet when the call of God came, they answered.

Moses was 80 years old when he was out there in the desert. For 40 years he had been there. He was a middle-aged man when he arrived, and yet God called him at the age of 80. A voice speaking out of that burning bush told him to go back to Egypt and say to the Pharaoh, "Let My people go."

There is an eternal formula that I have learned to apply to my own life. Once I submitted my life to Jesus Christ, from that time on I had voluntarily surrendered the right to choose, or the power to vary the consequences of that decision.

Moses had done that with his life. He had given it over to God and was waiting on the Lord. The word "wait" actually means to be entwined. It's like pieces of a rope that are all entwined together. Moses and God had become one, even though Moses didn't know His name.

Perhaps the greatest blessing is to be so unencumbered that when your bush burns and when God speaks, you can rise, and you can answer. Wait on God, because bushes still burn. God is still calling each one of us by name, no matter how old we may be or what our circumstances are.

Chapter 9

Hospitality: Learning to Give

Only in the wilderness does one learn that the best things in life really are free. As we journey with Moses through the wilderness, I want to teach you about the wonderful lesson of hospitality. Earlier, we visited the waters of Marah, sat on the roots of an ancient Acacia tree, climbed to where Moses struck the rock and brought forth water, looked out over the valley where Joshua defeated the Amalekites, held the rod of Moses, heard the grumblings of the Israelites over their changed diets, and most recently sat in the sand next to a bush that could have burst into flames at any minute.

Now, I want to talk to you about hospitality. In the desert, the essential things are always free. Water is free. No one is allowed to put a fence around a well. Shelter is free. Even your enemies are invited into your tent to escape the heat of the day. Fire is free, to warm yourself and to cook your meals. All of these things are to be shared.

On my last trip to the Sinai, I spent the night at a Bedouin cemetery, a place called Bir Igna — the grave of a man called Igna. In the cemetery there was a tomb of a sheik, an old Bedouin chieftain. We also discovered a Maqad, *a hospitality house, where we found, next to the tomb, a place where we could rest. There was also a well where we could fill our canteens.*

After we had packed our jeep the next morning, I asked my fellow travelers to gather as I taught them for a few minutes about hospitality.

The first reaction to any kind of wilderness experience is withdrawal. We experience the wilderness as we go through the pain of losing a loved one, or the shock of losing a job, or the betrayal of a friend. All of these things drive us into a wilderness where we want to withdraw. Frequently our first reaction is, "Leave me alone." And so we flee into a desert, a wilderness, where we can be alone.

Moses did that. He had killed an Egyptian taskmaster, only to find that God had something far better for him than simply fleeing into the desert. He was driven there, that's true; yet he immediately found that he had friends in the wilderness.

The very first night he spent in the wilderness, was at an oasis. There, he befriended the daughters of the Midian sheik, Jethro. They ran home to their father to tell him of their new Egyptian friend they had just met at the oasis. Jethro's reaction was, "Why did you leave him there alone? Invite him home to have something to eat." That always seems to be the reaction of the Bedouins in this place. They are a warm, open people of hospitality.

So Moses had his first Bedouin meal. He watched as Zipporah made what must have looked like pita bread — the flour and the water pasted together, then baked in the coals of the fire. Perhaps he heard Jethro speak that evening of the God they served, the God of Abraham, the God of no name, the God of no image. This was a God Moses knew very little about. And so here, in the desert with the hospitality of people that he had never met before, Moses began his position of preparation.

There's a code of hospitality among the desert people. Abraham was known as the father of hospitality. Abraham and Jethro came from the same kind of people. This code of hospitality says that no man should be left alone out in the desert. It's not right. Certain things in the desert are never denied, even to the enemy. Fire, for instance. Water, also. You'll never see a fence around a well. Shade from the harsh sun is always shared.

This was especially seen at Bir Igna as our guide showed us the Maqad, a place of hospitality. Inside, there was room for all who would come. Everyone was invited to enjoy the hospitality of the Maqad.

We found inside the Maqad various implements. We found a mortar with pestle, which had been left behind by a friendly Bedouin. There was a small teapot and some small cups to drink the hot seasoned tea in.

It's a lesson we all need to learn. It's the lesson of the wilderness. No matter how tough things are, no matter how dark things are, no matter how wild the desert or the wilderness becomes, God always sends us friends and those who will leave behind the things that we need.

Some things in the Sinai are free. The fire is free. The shade is free. The water is free. But mostly free is the lesson that we learn: God will always provide.

Chapter 10

The Law: Lessons from Mt. Sinai

Like most people, when I think of Mount Sinai, I automatically think of the Ten Commandments. Chiseled in stone and given to Moses as the basis for all law, nothing has so shaped the world of law and order as those Ten Commandments. When the Israelites left Egypt, they were nothing but a band of former slaves. God wanted them to become a nation of priests and kings. To bring them to maturity, God gave them The Law. It was given to Moses on Mount Sinai.

On each of my trips into the Sinai, the climax of the journey has been the climb up Mount Sinai, the mountain of Jebel Musa, as the Arabs call it. Each time, I've climbed up before dawn, climbing the steepest set in the early morning hours in order to reach the summit by sunrise. On my last trip, after reaching the top of the mountain, I stopped to teach about those Ten Commandments and about something I call the Eleventh Commandment.

We left Saint Catherine's Monastery hours before dawn. Climbing the steep sides of the granite mountain, we wanted to reach the summit before the sun came up. Every time I've been there, I've wondered how Moses must have felt as he left the children of Israel far below on the plain of *er Rakha* and climbed that mountain by himself to meet God.

We walked that same pathway that the children of Israel may have followed from the Gulf of Suez, along "the valley of the wind" called the *Naqb el Hawa*. It's the traditional "Pilgrim's Path" that ends at the plain of er Rakha, the place of rest. There the children of Israel camped, while Moses made his way up the mountain to hear God.

There in that awesome wilderness sanctuary, Moses was to receive a new revelation concerning the character of God. The children of Israel all knew of God. Up until that time they knew He was the God of no name, the God of no image, who talked to Moses. Now, they were about to discover a new and startling aspect of God's nature.

When God established His covenant with Abraham, He revealed Himself as *El Shaddai*, a term meaning simply "God Almighty." At the burning bush, He told Moses He was not only El Shaddai, the God of Abraham, Isaac and Jacob; He went on to say "I am that I am." At this point, God declared He was more than the essence of being, which is the root of the verb *I am*. He said He was the *cause* of being – underived existence coupled with an independent and uncontrolled will.

Then, on Mount Sinai, God revealed to Moses His true nature, not only by sharing His name, *Yahweh*, which was later translated "Jehovah," but by revealing His nature through The Law, those Ten Commandments.

During the march from Egypt to Mount Sinai, God spoke basically only to Moses, and then only on rare occasions. At the springs of Marah, the people heard Him; but the rest of the time, He was reflected in the pillar of cloud by day and in the column of fire by night. He was the God of no name and the God of no image. Then, one day, the God of history and the God of all existence made himself known. Bit by bit, in a process known as progressive revelation, God revealed Himself first to Moses, then to His people. He did it by giving them The Law, the Ten Commandments.

It seems strange that God would give commandments to people knowing that they couldn't keep them. The first High Priest, Aaron, broke the second commandment even before Moses got down from the mountain. Moses broke the third by misusing the name of God when he struck the rock rather than speaking to it as God had told him. Every one of the Ten Commandments was broken by the children of Israel before they left Mount Sinai, and we continue to break them even to this day. Now, if the Ten Commandments were impossible to keep, why did God give them?

God gave them to reveal His nature. God is far more interested in a people who want to establish a relationship with Him than He is in a people who keep all the rules but never learn to abide in His presence.

Perhaps this is best reflected in what I call the Eleventh Commandment. No sooner had God given His Ten Commandments to Moses did He began sharing some specific ordinances. These were rules for behavior to interpret the Ten Commandments. One of these ordinances had to do with the construction of altars. I call it the Eleventh Commandment. God said,

> "If you make an altar of stones for me, do not build it with dressed (or cut) stones, for you will defile it if you use a tool on it" (Exodus 20:25).

For many generations, the Israelites had been cutting stones in Egypt — stones to be used to make idols and in tombs, the pyramids of Egypt, where the pharaohs were buried. These were all made of hewn stones. The Hebrew slaves had spent all their last years making bricks in Egypt, shaped for the altars in Egypt. Now God was revealing a new plan. Jehovah, unlike all the Egyptian gods, did not need shaped stones. He didn't need man's efforts for acceptable worship. He preferred natural things, altars made of naturally shaped stones that had never been touched by hammer or chisel.

There's a sameness in bricks which is common to people who are in bondage. Bricks and hewn stones are made to conform. There's never any variation in them. All are made to fit exactly into a designated place with little or no irregularity, no originality. Slavery produces bricks; whether it's in the tone of the voice, the cut of the hair, or the vocabulary he uses, you can always tell a man who's in bondage, because he sounds and looks just like everybody else. Uniqueness is quenched, individuality is not allowed, genuine creativity is limited. The products all look like something produced yesterday, those used by everyone else.

Earlier, Moses had complained to God, saying that God had given him an army made of uncut stones. Not a single one of them seem to fit into place. On a number of occasions Moses wanted to chip them into shape, to conform them to the image he felt they should take. Each time God said, "Hands off, Moses. I'll do it. It's My job to conform each man to the shape I want him to have. I am the master builder who fits each stone into its place."

The wilderness teaches us that God is not as much interested in rules as He is in relationships. Sure, God puts limitations on us, but He uses uncut stones. As we walk to spiritual maturity, we take our eyes off the rules of the bricks and realize that God wants to fit each one of us into place.

The Israelites were now free. The problem is they became free-wheeling. God, therefore, put restrictions around them — rules, not to destroy them, but to channel them to use their creativity and make them productive. So God brought the people to Himself and showed them that, in order to have complete freedom, they had to be a people under authority. True happiness really comes when we're submitted to God and submitted to each other.

Later in God's history, we find The Law was not supposed to be an end, but a means to a greater end. The Ten Commandments, although not to be flaunted, were given to reveal the nature of God.

If all we do is try to keep the rules, we'll forever be in slavery. But if we use the rules to move in closer to God, then we will discover that the laws are not chains to hold us down; they're guideposts to reveal the nature of God and to set us free.

Many centuries later the Apostle Peter said,

> As you come to him, the living Stone – rejected by men but chosen by God and precious to him – you also, like living stones, are being built into a spiritual house to be a holy priesthood, offering spiritual sacrifices acceptable to God through Jesus Christ (1 Peter 2:4-5).

Chapter 11

Pilgrims: Staying Under the Cloud

Throughout this booklet we've been following the footsteps of Moses through the Sinai. As we have traveled, I hope you've been moving towards spiritual maturity. I hope that you're closer to God now than you were when we started.

The blowing of the shofar — the sounding of the ram's horn — is a signal to come up higher. It's a call to worship, a sound to be up and moving. One of the important lessons we need to learn in the wilderness, as we move toward spiritual maturity, is the fact that we're all pilgrims. That was one of the first lessons God taught the children of Israel: the lesson of staying under the cloud.

God knew it would be easy for those former slaves to settle down the first chance they got and get comfortable in the wilderness. Therefore, the first order of business was to keep them moving. How can you reach your goal to spiritual maturity if you're not on the move? A friend of mine once told me that he joined a church, and the pastor said to him, "Have a seat." He said he's been doing that ever since.

You see, you'll never reach spiritual maturity if you remain seated on your journey to maturity. When we speak of the Holy Spirit, we speak of the movements of the Holy Spirit. In the wilderness, the Israelites were told to keep their eye on the cloud, and to stay under it as it moved.

Now, join us at special location high on the side of Mount Sinai. It's a place where the old hermits had their caves during the fourth and fifth centuries. It overlooks Saint Catherine's Monastery, 2000 feet below. Here, I taught about the ram's horn, about the danger of being a hermit, and about the necessity of being a pilgrim moving through the wilderness toward the Promise Land.

At the 6,000 foot level on Mount Sinai, high above Saint Catherine's Monastery, there is a little place called a *farsh*, which is actually a high mountain oasis. There, one can fill canteens and take a rest. The water tastes good high up on the mountain. There is an interesting thing about this place; it is where Elijah came as he was fleeing from Jezebel.

Yet, the question so many ask after being in the desert, after going through the wilderness experience, and even after entering the promised land of salvation and a Spirit-filled life, is, "Why do we so often find ourselves back in the wilderness?" Perhaps the reason we ask this question is because we misunderstand what exactly the "Promised Land" is.

The wilderness is really not a bad place to live. I've discovered this as I have made many trips to the Sinai. A person can live there and live rather comfortably for long periods of time. The children of Israel were there, and it was a good place for them. Sure, they were out of the will of God and they were wandering, but they had free food every morning, manna from heaven. Their clothes didn't wear out. Their shoes didn't wear out. They were protected from the snakes. It was a pretty good place to be.

Wildernesses are like that, and there's always a temptation to want to stay there rather than to move on into the Promised Land. Why? Because the Promised Land must be taken. Yes, salvation is free. We understand that. It's a gift of God. It's God's grace. But our salvation has to be worked out. The Promised Land has to be worked out. When the Israelites finally made it to the Promised Land, they still had to fight the giants of Anak and capture the walled cities.

Perhaps that's the meaning of the *farsh* high on Mount Sinai. The prophet Elijah had tasted of the Promised Land. He lived in the Promised Land. Then, suddenly, he found himself forced back into the wilderness. He'd had a great victory at Mount Carmel, when he'd overcome the priests of Baal as fire came down from heaven and consumed them. But the very next day he was fleeing for his life. Eventually he came to that *farsh* high on the mountain of God. And when he got there, exhausted, he began to doubt his own purpose for being, his own salvation. What in the world was a man who had tasted of the Promised Land doing back in the wilderness?

It was there, just below the summit of Mount Sinai, that God spoke again to Elijah. The words of John Keble (1792-1866) come to mind when I think of that:

> On Horeb, with Elijah, let us lie,
> Where all around, on mountain, sand, and sky,
> God's chariot-wheels have left distinctest trace.

Maybe that's the reason for the wildernesses in our lives — so that we can see God's chariot wheels, the place where God has been. Hear again the still, small voice as it speaks to you, as it did to Elijah after he came from that place of great victory.

There is such a tendency inside each and every one of us to want to see the sensational, to want to see the hand of God. And yet God is not so interested in revealing His hand as He is in wanting us to see His face and hear His voice. So the purpose of the *farsh*, the high mountain oasis, is so we can get quiet and stop, be refreshed, and listen for the voice of God.

God spoke again to Elijah as he was laying in that quiet place. There was a strong wind. There was an earthquake. There was a great fire. Yet, God was not in any of that. It was only when all of that had passed that God spoke in a still, small voice. Hear His voice again, today, quiet and soft, at the *farsh*.

Chapter 12

Faith: Lessons from Kadesh Barnea

Our journey is almost over, and we've learned some valuable lessons about spiritual maturity. We've studied purging, provision, obedience, authority, changed appetites, restoration, the call of God, hospitality, the living commandments, and the pilgrims.

Now, I want us to visit another desert oasis in the northern Sinai, a place called Kadesh Barnea. It was there, after a year and a half of wandering, that the children of Israel came before their final push into the Promised Land. But something happened at Kadesh Barnea — something tragic. Instead of pushing on and possessing the land God had given them, they were destined to wander in the desert for another 38 years until all the grumblers, all the complainers, all those who were without faith, had died.

On my last trip into the Sinai, I sat one day beside a small palm tree at Kadesh Barnea. It was there that I taught a lesson about faith. I hope it will stimulate you as you broaden your study on the lessons of spiritual maturity — and on the lessons of life as well.

It is a journey of several days from Mount Sinai to a beautiful little oasis at Kadesh Barnea, in the northern part of the Sinai peninsula. It was there that God had intended for the children of Israel to regroup, to feed their flocks, and then to go in and take the land He had promised them. In fact, from that place, you can literally see the borders of the Promised Land. Moses however, was approached by a delegation, representatives of the people, who came to him and said, "Don't you think it would be a good idea if we sent some spies into the land before we go across to take it?"

Watch out for good ideas! This was not part of God's original plan. God intended for the people to march forward, under the cloud, under the anointing, and take the land. They had already come 400 miles in about 15 months. Surely they had learned by now that God was faithful, that He could be trusted, and that if He asked them to do anything He would also provide the means to accomplish that which He asked.

But instead of moving out with the morning's light, the people hesitated. It was the first step toward unbelief.

You see, instead of acting by faith and believing God, they grew cautious. They were afraid there would be giants in the land, walled cities, or obstacles too great for them to overcome. Well, sure enough, they received what they confessed. Their refusal to believe, their negative faith, brought about their downfall.

Faith marches ahead when God speaks. But the Israelites were not able to enter the Promised Land because of their unbelief. Instead, they sent their 12 spies in, one from each tribe. Of these 12 we know the names of only two. Caleb, who wholly followed the Lord, and Joshua, who was called the minister of Moses.

The spies left Kadesh Barnea near the end of July, making a long route up through the Promised Land, then coming back down through the Negev Desert, stopping at a place called Hebron. Someplace along the way in one of the valleys, they had cut a bunch of grapes. They were so heavy it took two men to carry them, slung on a staff over their shoulders. They gathered pomegranates and figs and brought them back. After about 40 days, they returned to the camp and showed all of their wares.

But there was a majority negative report amongst the spies. Only Joshua and Caleb were positive. Most of the spies said, "We can't do it. Sure, the land flows with milk and honey, but you ought to see the people who live there. The cities are fortified, and the folks look like the descendants of Anak, the giants. We seem like grasshoppers in our own eyes, and we look the same in their eyes as well."

It seems that people love to hear a negative report. The human heart loves to be deceived. It loves to rebel against God. It's the nature of man to be careful, to be faithless. The spies looked and saw themselves as grasshoppers. Joshua and Caleb, however, looked at God and saw they could overcome.

The people, however, sided with the negative report. The obstacles were too great to overcome. But in their decision, they made a fatal mistake. Unbelief never sees beyond the difficulties. It always looks at the walled cities and the giants rather than looking at God.

Faith looks at God. Unbelief looks at obstacles. Now, faith does not minimize the danger of the difficulties, but it says God is big enough to overcome them. The Israelites, standing on the verge of the Promised Land, looked inward. They saw themselves as grasshoppers. They tried to imagine how the giants would see them, and they saw more grasshoppers. They failed to do the one thing that Joshua and Caleb had done: they failed to look at God.

The results of their decision were tragic. Because of their disobedience, their unbelief, God told them they were going to remain in the desert for 38 years until the whole generation of unbelievers died — until every faithless man and woman was buried in the ground. Then, and then only, would Moses, Joshua, and Caleb — those who had remained faithful — be allowed to start the march towards the Promised Land. In the long run, only Joshua and Caleb were able to enter the Promised Land.

The road of faith constantly takes us through the wilderness. It's a lonely road. Joshua and Caleb walked that road, and because of that, they had to spend time in the desert with the faithless ones. Yet, it is the road toward spiritual maturity, always leading through the wilderness. In the wilderness God allows us to understand the circumstances. He will strip us of all the things that we have, and we will see the meaninglessness of material possessions.

In the wilderness, we will find out that God alone can be trusted. It is then, as we make preparations for the final days, God will say, "Now, I will show you My glory," and liberate us to glory.

It's so easy to think that you're a grasshopper when you're standing against the knees of a giant. Yet, faith says God is bigger than the giants of this world.

In the last stanza of Robert Frost's poem, "The Road Not Taken," he writes,

> I shall be telling this with a sigh,
> somewhere ages and ages hence:
> Two roads diverged in a wood, and I –
> I took the one less travelled by,
> And that has made all the difference.

Joshua and Caleb took the road less traveled by. The others, more cautious, chose the broad way. Because of that, their bones are buried in the sands at Kadesh Barnea. And yet, God raised up a new generation of young Israelis, brave men and women who were willing to follow those men of faith and take the land God had promised their fathers.

No longer did they see themselves as grasshoppers. They saw themselves for who they really were — the children of God. That's the message of faith.

Jamie Buckingham

Chapter 13

Relationships: The Family of God

We have reached the last chapter in our study of the journey to spiritual maturity. We've come a long way from the waters of Marah, through the Sinai, south to Elim, then through the Valley of Rephidim to Mount Sinai itself. From there we traced the footsteps of Moses north, until we wound up at Kadesh Barnea. That was also the last stop for the children of Israel before eventually entering the Promised Land.

I've traced the footsteps of Moses a number of times over the past several years. Each time I've taken a small group of men with me, and each time we've prayed ahead of time that during our two-week camping trip, God would form us into a church, a family, real brothers in the Lord. And each time God was faithful.

In this final chapter I want to discuss one of the most important lessons to be learned in the wilderness, one of the most important lessons of spiritual maturity: the necessity of forming relationships, of being loyal to one another.

As I and my small group of pilgrims concluded our trip through the desert, we came upon a place in the north where the mountains were no longer granite. They were sandstone. We sat to rest in the shade overlooking a great valley below. In just a few days, we would be back in the United States. Each of us would go to our individual homes and resume our regular activities. But we knew that in that great crucible of the wilderness, God had formed us into a family. We were brothers. We would never be the same. We would always be friends.

That final day in the desert was a special time in our lives. It was a time to reflect on our shared experiences and the formation of our deep and lasting relationships with each other.

We've been more than eight days making our way through the wilderness and one of the things we've all discovered is the necessity of huddling. At night, when the rocks get cold and the wind whistles down the deep wadis, when the only shade that we can find is some kind of overhanging rock, there's a real necessity to draw together.

One of the things we've learned in the wilderness is that there are only a few genuinely habitable places — and maybe that's the way it should be. Because the wilderness is not a place to settle. It's a place for us to pass through. To live apart, however, means that we die. So we learn to come together. We learn to huddle together, and the wilderness breeds a certain degree of loyalty.

What has happened over the days and nights out in the Sinai is we've been forced into a deep camaraderie of covenant relationship. We've learned to take care of each other. We've learned to give way to each other. We've learned things about each other that we would never know back in the civilized world we came from. The wilderness tends to bring people together. It's not a bad place, after all, as long as we don't dwell here, live here, stay here — as long as we are on the move.

Covenant in its purest form is a binding, solemn agreement toward some kind of common goal. We've found some common goals while traveling through the desert. But things that grow out of conflict are always tested by suffering.

Moses entered into covenant with God, and then God entered into covenant with the people of Israel as they passed through the desert places. One of the covenants that Moses described to the children of Israel was the ancient covenant of salt. In fact, he said in the book of Leviticus,

> Season all your grain offerings with salt. Do not leave
> the salt of the covenant of your God out of your grain
> offerings; add salt to all your offerings" (Leviticus
> 2:13).

In the desert places, we learned to enter into covenant with one another. When the Bedouin make bread in the desert, they take flour, add water, and then they add salt. Salt is still part of the food eaten here. The bread has salt.

Covenant people are people who have entered into the covenant of salt. The Bedouin are a covenant people. They have a saying, "There's salt among us," which signifies that they are a people of loyalty.

This is how the genuine church should be. We ought to be a people of loyalty. Even though it wasn't planned, one of the things that happened to me and my friends in the wilderness was that we became a church. We became a people who are loyal to one another. We are people with a mission. We are going someplace. We're under authority. That's what the church really is — a group of people who've entered into the covenant of salt. So we could say to each other, "There's salt among us." We are that kind of people.

Jesus had a saying that He used in the Sermon on the Mount. He said, "You are the salt of the earth." Most of us have heard a number of sermons on what salt does. It preserves. It purifies. It does many, many things. Yet, I don't think that's what Jesus was talking about at all. I think Jesus was talking about the fact that we, as the church, are a group of people who've entered into covenant relationship. And if we lose that covenant relationship, then we, "the salt of the earth," have lost our savor, and we're good for nothing.

If we have to be bound together through formal memberships or through any other kind of outward sign, then we're really not a people of covenant. A grain of salt may disappear. But as people of salt, we continue on.

Salt is made up of two ingredients, sodium and chloride. Either one taken separately is poison. But put those ingredients together and what is created — salt — constitutes a covenant relationship that extends life, and gives savor to those around us. That is what happened in the desert. Relationships, salt covenants, were formed that will last forever — and in the process they bring life.

Jamie Buckingham

The following is the first chapter in Jamie Buckingham's book A Way Through the Wilderness, *which provides a more in-depth study on the topic of spiritual growth. It can be found at www.RLMin.com.*

A Way Through the Wilderness

Hospitality

"And where is he?" [Jethro] asked his daughters. "Why did you leave him? Invite him to have something to eat" (Exodus 2:20).

The first reaction to any wilderness is withdrawal. The pain of losing a loved one, the shock of losing a job, the deep disappointment of being betrayed by someone you love – all tend to drive us into deep withdrawal.

Invariably our first reaction is, "Leave me alone."

God understands this. He also understands our even greater need to be part of a family – to be touched by loving hands, held by loving arms. Thus, into every wilderness experience of ours, God sends special messengers to minister to us. To Jesus He sent angels. To Elijah He sent ravens. To Moses He sent an old Bedouin sheikh.

Jethro, with warm, simple hospitality, helped the former prince of Egypt emerge from his shell of grief and self-pity and enter a world of preparation, a world designed by God to train him for the time he would return to Egypt for a far greater purpose.

Moses, at age 40, had been second-in-command in the most powerful and academically advanced nation of history. As an infant, he had been rescued from the sword of Pharaoh and raised by Pharaoh's daughter as a prince. Trained in courtly manners and given the best education available, his foster mother looked for the day when Moses would replace her father on the throne of Egypt.

But God had other plans, plans that could come to pass only after the egotism of Egypt had been burned from His servant in the crucible of the wilderness.

It began, as most wilderness wanderings begin, with an act of sin. In the Egyptian province of Goshen, where the Hebrew slaves were toiling in the blistering sun making bricks in the stiff clay pits, Moses killed an Egyptian taskmaster who was whipping a defenseless Hebrew slave.

It was a chivalrous act, well-meant, springing largely from human sympathy. Ironically, it was one of the first genuinely unselfish things Moses had done. At the same time, it was an act of murder, and the consequences were swift and merciless.

In his own strength, Moses was not strong enough to lead. So, using the justice of the Egyptians, God did something that still mystifies mortal man: He began the process of spiritual education by thrusting Moses into the great and terrible wilderness of the Sinai. Here he learned to distinguish between passion and principle, between impulse and settled purpose. Only in the wilderness does one learn that mere need never constitutes a call. One learns to wait on the voice of God.

Formal education is only the beginning of spiritual preparation. At the age of 40, Moses entered God's graduate school. The next forty years were spent in the deprivation of the wilderness. These were years in which his rough edges were sanded smooth. The literal blast furnace of the Sinai refined the character of a man God was going to use. There he learned to pray and he learned the values of solitude. There, starting with a few sheep and goats, he learned the principles of leadership. But he did not have to struggle alone. God put a family around him – the family of Jethro – who taught him the ways of the desert people, the ways of hospitality.

Moses had been into the Sinai before, but always as a military commander, never as a solitary pilgrim. There is evidence he may have led at least one expedition as far south as Dophkah, where the remains of an ancient Egyptian temple still stand at the site of the turquoise mines near Serabit el Khadim. But viewing the desert from a pharaoh's chariot is much different from viewing it as a lonely sojourner in exile, plodding through the sand and clambering over the rocks: a man who had lost not only his country but his family as well.

Filled with despair and confusion, the once prince of Egypt staggered into the burning crucible of the wilderness.

Making his way across the peninsula to nowhere, he began his wanderings. Awed by the blood-red sky at dawn, the star-studded cover of the night canopy, by the gaunt face of a primeval crag, by the vast emptiness, by the seemingly endless stretch of burning sand, he stumbled on until he came to an oasis. Exhausted, he drank from the pool of water, then fell into the shade and slept. He was awakened by human voices speaking the ancient language still spoken by the old Israelites in the slave quarters of Egypt.

Young maidens, Bedouin girls in their early and mid-teens, had come to water their father's flocks. Shepherds from other tribes were at the oasis also. Recognizing the girls as strangers in the area, they were driving them away. Still angry from everything that had happened to him, Moses emerged from the shadows to strike out at the shepherd bullies. His wooden staff swinging, he charged at them, prepared to do to them what he had done to the Egyptian taskmaster. They fled, and the shepherd girls, grateful, once again drove their flocks to the water at the pool.

Giggling and hiding behind their veils, they returned to the nearby tent of their father, the Bedouin sheikh called Jethro (also called Reuel) who had moved his tribe from the territory southeast of Aqaba to forage in the Sinai.

"Why did you leave him?" Jethro quizzed his daughters. "Invite him to have something to eat."

That night Moses sat in the tent of Jethro and ate his first wilderness meal. He was about to learn the first of many wilderness lessons.

Sitting in the tiny *succoth*, or thatched hut made of date palm leaves, Moses watched, fascinated, as Jethro's beautiful young daughter Zipporah ground grain brought with them from Midian. Two large round stones were placed on top of each other. The bottom stone had a small trough around the edge. The top stone had a wooden handle affixed to one side so it could be turned on an axle that joined both stones in the middle. The maiden slowly poured the grain through a hole in the top stone, at the same time turning the stone so that the grain was crushed between the stones. The flour was collected in the small trough at the edge.

When there was enough, Zipporah added water and salt to the flour, kneaded it into a dough ball about the size of a grapefruit, then patted it out into large flat cakes about an inch thick. Next Zipporah laid the cake – called *libre*[1]– directly onto the glowing coals made from dried camel dung. Watching carefully to see it did not char, she then flipped it over so the baked side was on top. Scraping up sand and ashes, she covered the entire cake, coals and all.

In a few moments her mother arrived with a huge dish of boiled mutton and herbs that had been cooking in another booth. Zipporah then brushed the sand from the bread and, holding it between her hands, slapped it with both hands in a clapping motion, knocking off sand and char.

Jethro motioned for the family to be seated, cross legged in a circle around the fire. Moses sat next to the sheikh as the honored guest. Before eating they prayed. It was a strange experience for Moses. There were no images, no idols, just the mention of an unknown God, "El."

---

[1] This same bread, when cooked on a piece of metal laid over the coals, is called *fatir*. It is similar to the modern pita bread, though it is thinner and does not have a double crust, or pocket. It is often cooked over dried camel dung, small pellets about the size of charcoal briquettes, which burn like charcoal.

"Who is this El?" Moses asked. "Is He like the sun god Re, the river god *Osiris*, or *Hathor* whom the Egyptians worship at Dophkah?"

"I have heard of these false gods," Jethro replied, tearing off a piece of bread and dipping it into the stew bowl. "El is higher than them all. There are no gods but Him. El is at the center of all being. He spoke in times past to our father Abraham. Your ancestor Jacob bought a parcel of land for one hundred pieces of silver at Shechem in Canaan and set up an altar to El, whom he called *El Elohe* or *El Elyon*, the Most High God."

"I have heard that story from my mother in Egypt, but none of my people know the name of that god. It has long been forgotten. They know Him only as the god with no name and no image – the god of Abraham, Isaac and Jacob."

Jethro smiled and nodded. "I, too, am a son of Abraham. My ancestor, Midian – the fourth son of Abraham by Mother Keturah – was sent away into the east country. Our people tell of a visit by El to Father Abraham when he was one hundred less one. El changed his name from Abram, exalted father, to Abraham, father of many. Abraham then called El by the name of *El Shaddai* – God Almighty. He and all the males in his household were circumcised as a sign of the covenant that is yet to be fulfilled."

Moses sat long into the night, listening to the fascinating stories of Jethro. It is easy to learn from a man of hospitality.

This unwritten code of hospitality is still practiced in the Sinai. It is a code that originated with Abraham, whom Jew and Muslim both call "Father of Hospitality." It was Abraham who first decreed that the essentials of life were never to be denied any wilderness pilgrim, be he friend or enemy.

In Genesis 18, Abraham was approached by three strangers as he camped at Mamre. Sitting at the entrance to his tent, the childless, discouraged old nomad, the first of the Bedouins, saw the men approaching across the desert. He quickly brought them water to drink, then provided the extra luxury of water to wash their feet. Finally he offered them the shade of his tree.

The tree, mentioned in Genesis 18:4 and later in verse 8, is known as an *eshel*, or tamarisk, tree. After the wayfarers had eaten and been refreshed, they blessed Abraham by announcing Sarah would have a child. The Jewish Talmud says Abraham then responded by saying, "Now bless him of whose bounty ye have eaten. Think not it is of mine ye have eaten. No, it is of Him who spoke and the world was created."

One of the old Talmudic sages explains that *eshel* actually means a hospice, and consists of the initial letters of the three words that indicated hospitality: *achila* (food), *shetiya* (drink) and *lina* (accommodation for the night).

After the treaty with Abimelech, the Philistine chieftain, Abraham planted a tamarisk (*eshel*) tree in Beersheba (Genesis 21:33) to remind all who passed that way of the bond of hospitality among desert people. Ever since, the wells, the fire and the shade have belonged to all mankind.

There is no greater pleasure for the Bedouin than that of offering hospitality. Welcoming travelers is at the core of desert culture and is performed even if it means sharing the last piece of bread . . .

Spiritual Maturity

Jamie Buckingham

ABOUT JAMIE BUCKINGHAM

A master storyteller and Bible teacher, Jamie Buckingham has delighted millions around the world both in person and in print.

He wrote more than 45 books, including biographies of some of this century's best known Christians, including Pat Robertson (*Shout It from the Housetops*), Corrie ten Boom (*Tramp for the Lord* and others), and Kathryn Kuhlman (*Daughter of Destiny, God Can Do it Again* and others). His other biographies include the national bestseller *Run Baby Run* (with Nicky Cruz), *From Harper Valley to the Mountaintop* (with Jeannie C. Riley), and *O Happy Day* (the Happy Goodman Family Singers). Other books by Jamie Buckingham include *Risky Living*; *Where Eagles Soar*; *A Way Through the Wilderness*; *Miracle Power*; *Coping With Criticism; Into The Glory; 10 Miracles of Jesus;; The Nazarene; 10 Parables of Jesus; The Last Word; The Truth Will Set You Free...But First It Will Make You Miserable;* and *Jesus World* (a novel).

He also wrote *Power for Living*, a book sponsored by the Arthur DeMoss Foundation that was given away to millions of people worldwide and resulted in untold numbers of people coming to Christ.

Jamie was more than an author of books. He was an award-winning columnist for *Charisma Magazine* and served as Editor-in-Chief of *Ministries Today Magazine* until his death in February 1992. A popular conference speaker, he was recognized as one of America's foremost authorities on the Sinai and Israel. He wrote and produced more than 100 video teachings on location in the Holy Land.

As a distinguished Bible teacher with graduate degrees in English Literature and Theology, Jamie was respected among liturgical, evangelical, and Pentecostal Christians. He was considered a close friend and confidant of many key Christians of the late 20th century, including Oral Roberts, Billy Graham, Catherine Marshall, Jack Hayford, Bob Mumford, Kathryn Kuhlman, Corrie ten Boom, John Sherrill, Bill Bright, John Hagee, Pat Robertson, and many others.

Most importantly, Jamie was a husband, father, grandfather, and founding pastor of the Tabernacle Church, an interdenominational congregation in Melbourne, Florida, where he served for 25 years, pastoring and discipling followers of Christ. He lived in a rural area on the east coast of Florida on a family compound with his wife, Jackie, surrounded by five married children and 14 grandchildren.

For more information on Jamie Buckingham, please visit www.JamieBuckinghamMinistries.com. Many of his books, columns, additional writings, video devotional series, and audio and video sermons can be found on this website, which is dedicated to preserving and promoting his life works.

Jamie Buckingham

For more of Jamie Buckingham's books, teachings and video devotionals, or if you would like additional copies of this book, go to:

www.JamieBuckinghamMinistries.com

You can us on Facebook.

Risky Living Ministries, Inc.

www.RLMin.com

Made in the USA
Monee, IL
07 November 2021